CHiLD SOLDiER
When Boys and Girls Are Used in War

WRITTEN BY **Jessica Dee Humphreys & Michel Chikwanine**

ILLUSTRATED BY **Claudia Dávila**

CitizenKid™

A collection of books that inform children about the
world and inspire them to be better global citizens

KIDS CAN PRESS

To my mother, for *Mermaids* and the *OED* — JDH

To the African heroes whose inspiration and spirit go unheard ...
and yet are the most powerful — MC

To Michael, who inspires me every day — CD

My name is Michel Chikwanine. The story you are about to read is true. It is my story, and it is just one of thousands like it. But I want you to know that these events did not occur out of the blue and won't suddenly happen to you. Many years of war, poverty and desperation passed before people in my country resorted to the use of child soldiers.

Peering through the airport window, I watched the white flakes floating gently through the dark sky.

We'd finally arrived in North America. I'd been told the streets here were so clean you could walk outside in your socks. I had hoped to try it as soon as we landed, but the pilot said it was 42 degrees below zero outside. I wondered how people survived here.

Then I looked up at the snow softly falling. There were no bullets. There were no bombs.

I felt happy again. It had been a long, long time.

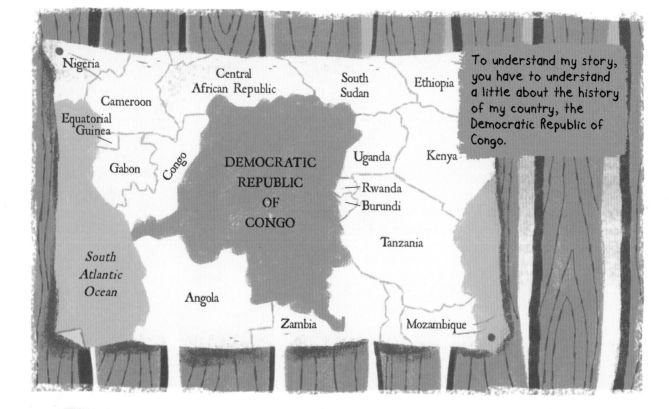

To understand my story, you have to understand a little about the history of my country, the Democratic Republic of Congo.

Nigeria

Central African Republic

South Sudan

Ethiopia

Cameroon

Equatorial Guinea

Gabon

Congo

DEMOCRATIC REPUBLIC OF CONGO

Uganda

Kenya

Rwanda

Burundi

Tanzania

South Atlantic Ocean

Angola

Zambia

Mozambique

My homeland is one of the most bountiful in the world. The earth is filled to the brim with minerals such as diamonds and gold; the rainforests are thick with plants, fruits and animals.

Sadly, these resources have also been its curse. For hundreds of years, greed has driven people to Central Africa to take — not share — this wealth.

Generations ago, the king of Belgium decided he wanted this land and its natural riches for himself. He did not care about the people who lived there except to use them as slaves. More than half the population was killed during his reign.

Eventually, after almost a hundred years, the Congolese people had had enough. In 1960, the country achieved independence after a long struggle. But by then everyone had grown up under Belgian rule, and no one knew how to go back to the old ways. Congolese men were brought into power, each promising a better life for their people. But these leaders only cared about making things better for themselves.

LIBÉRATION!

For decades, constant war and conflict made the region unstable, insecure and dangerous. Attempts at peace failed. But through it all, people still enjoyed their lives — they worked, they studied, they visited with friends. And, like anywhere, children played.

However, by 1993, when my story begins, things were about to get a whole lot worse.

I was five years old. There were rumblings of chaos growing in the distance, but I didn't hear them. I played soccer, I watched TV, I went to school, and I daydreamed.

We lived in the lush green hills of Beni, near a long, dusty road that led to a market in the center of town, where my mom sold fish and beautiful fabric called *bikwembe*.

My mom also shopped there for our dinner. Often I'd go with her and watch her haggle.

TWO DOLLARS.

I'LL GIVE YOU ONE FIFTY.

NO, NO!

FINE. GOOD-BYE.

OKAY, OKAY, ONE SEVENTY-FIVE.

ONE THIRTY!

She was tough, my mom.

Children in Beni would often spend their free time gathering scraps of paper and plastic bags to make soccer balls. We'd crumple the paper and wrap layer after layer of plastic bags around it. Then we'd twist dried banana leaves into string and tie it all up.

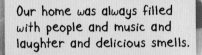

Our home was always filled with people and music and laughter and delicious smells.

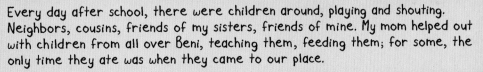

Every day after school, there were children around, playing and shouting. Neighbors, cousins, friends of my sisters, friends of mine. My mom helped out with children from all over Beni, teaching them, feeding them; for some, the only time they ate was when they came to our place.

My older sisters, Vicky and Viviane, helped my mom run the house. My little sister, Marizia, was the baby. All my sisters thought they were extra special, but I knew the truth. When I grew up, I would take care of everyone! I would be just like my dad, and that was SOMETHING!

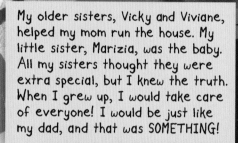

THIS IS MICHEL'S TIME.

Dad and I shared tea in the mornings; that was for him and me alone.

My dad was huge, so tall he towered over everyone. He was a human rights lawyer and always fought for what was right. He was respected, and he was feared. Yet he was incredibly compassionate. And he was always on my side, even when I was in trouble, which was a lot of the time.

Looking back, I see it was unfair that I had been raised to think I was great because of my gender instead of my deeds. But Congo, like most of the world, suffers from "boy is best" thinking. Although my dad was smart, modern and understanding, he was still a product of his upbringing and his culture. I guess we all are.

I would sit close beside my dad while we listened to the news on the radio. He told me about the world, and though I didn't understand half of it, I loved being near him and being special to him.

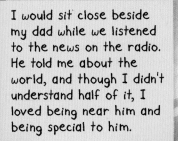

HA HA, CHICKENS!

As the only boy in the family, I was kind of spoiled. Maybe that's why I liked breaking rules and pushing buttons. Or maybe it was because I wanted to be like my dad, who was always taking a stand.

Whatever the reason, I'd often try to challenge kids bigger than me. Usually, they wouldn't fight back. Not because they were afraid of me, but because I was little — though I didn't realize that then.

With my father on my side, I was fearless.

I see now that I could be bratty. I was small and favored, so I acted tougher than I was. Who knew that tough act would soon save my life?

Early one Friday morning, I was getting ready for school, washing my face with the water my sisters had collected the night before.

They were yelling at me to hurry, when my dad pulled me aside. His face was stern.

BE HOME BY SIX, MICHEL.

OKAY, OKAY...

Coming straight home after school was one of the biggest rules in our house, and the one most tempting to break.

I tried to edge away, anxious to meet my friend Kevin on the road.

MICHEL! YOU COME STRAIGHT HOME FROM SCHOOL, UNDERSTAND ME?

I WANT TO SEE YOU WALK THROUGH THIS DOOR AT SIX O'CLOCK!

NDIYO, PAPA.

I ran as fast as I could to catch up with Kevin.

He was twelve and I was five, but he was my best friend. We were born in the same hospital, in the same month, seven years apart. Our moms sold *bikwembe* together, and we were like brothers.

As we walked, I thought about my dad's words. The hours of sunlight in Congo are long, so school starts at seven in the morning and ends at five in the afternoon. It took an hour to walk home. But today was Friday, and Kevin and I had planned to play soccer after school.

When we got to the schoolyard, Kevin headed off to the Fifth Year room, calling over his shoulder to me, *"Á plus tard!"*

We spoke Swahili at home, as well as our local and ancestral languages Lingala, Mashi and Kinande. But ever since Belgian colonization, Congolese kids could only speak French at school, even in the yard. Breaking that rule meant a smack with the willow switch — another holdover from Belgian rule.

When the bell finally rang that day, I stayed put, thinking again about my dad.

If I left now, he'd be pleased I did as I was told and we'd have ice cream from the shop in Butembo. I knew he'd be angry if I came home late.

Oh, that's just Dad fussing, I finally decided. I raced out to the field.

We were playing half-pitch: whoever scored a goal then had to go in net. Most of the kids tried not to score, but not me. I swooped down and kicked the ball straight in.

GOOOOAL!

Running to take my place as goalie, I noticed several army trucks pulling up.

Growing up, we often saw military vehicles and uniformed soldiers. Our president, a terrible dictator, had stopped paying his army. He told them: if you want money, go get it. So they introduced a curfew, and anyone caught outside after 7 p.m. would be stopped by soldiers and robbed. It was unfair, but there was nothing anyone could do about it.

Because it was still early and these trucks were so common, I didn't pay any attention to them. Until we heard a loud

BANG!!

We all fell to the ground in shock. A group of men ran toward us carrying machine guns and shouting.

We had never seen soldiers like these before. They had red eyes and scruffy hair; they were wearing shabby T-shirts over ragged jeans and cheap rain boots.

At first, I thought this had to be a joke.

We found out later that they were members of some kind of rebel militia — people trained as soldiers but who fight against the army instead of for it. This was one of many groups starting to spring up at that time, but we children knew nothing about this.

HOW OLD ARE YOU, EIGHT?

GET OVER THERE!

Yelling, they pointed their guns and used them to push us up one at a time.

YOU, THIRTEEN? OVER THERE!

When one of the rebel soldiers came toward me, I jumped up in front of him. I glared into his face and shouted.

MY NAME IS MICHEL CHIKWANINE. I AM FIVE YEARS OLD, AND IF MY FATHER FINDS OUT WHAT YOU ARE DOING, HE WILL PUNISH YOU!

He burst out laughing and hit me across the face with his gun.

I realized then that this was no joke.

I was thrown into the back of a truck with several other boys and driven into the hills. I was so scared. Kevin was in another truck. I couldn't talk to him. I couldn't even see him.

When the truck stopped, we were ordered to get out. I heard a crunch underneath my feet. It was a skeleton without its skull. I panicked, and my legs couldn't move. The smell in the air was disgusting.

When all the kids were out of the trucks, a rebel soldier shot at the ground in front of us. Terrified, we ran toward the nearby trees to hide. But when we got there, another soldier jumped out and started shooting at the ground, too. We stopped, not knowing where to run next.

I didn't know what to do, so I just started screaming.

RAT-
TAT-
TAT-
TAT!

It had been a test. The soldiers began to pull kids who had run slowly to one side, the fast ones to the other.

They used their guns to push the kids on my side into the long grass. I thought we were all going to be shot.

Instead, they lined us up.

WE ARE GOING TO INITIATE YOU INTO OUR ARMY!

They grabbed our struggling arms. The rebel soldier who had hit me used a long, jagged knife to cut my wrist and rubbed powder into the wound.

They called it Brown Brown — a mixture of gunpowder and a drug called cocaine. Right away I began to feel like my brain was trying to jump out of my head.

Would I be whipped? I braced myself and held my hands out. Everything was swirling in my brain, and my legs were shaking so hard I thought my knees would buckle.

Something heavy was dropped into my arms, but it fell to the ground with a thump. The rebel soldier put it right into my hands. It was a gun. Someone else was behind me and grabbed my fingers, putting one on the trigger.

SHOOT!
SHOOT!

YOUR FAMILY WILL NEVER TAKE YOU BACK NOW. WE ARE YOUR ONLY FAMILY.

They took off my blindfold.
My hands were shaking hard.

Kevin was lying in front of me in a pool of blood.
I had been forced to kill my best friend.

The next morning, I woke up with my head pounding and spinning. I could hear children crying.

WAKE UP!

Suddenly, all around us were gunshots, stomping boots and shouting.

I stayed curled up on the ground. I felt helpless. I felt dead. I lay there crying.

Someone sat down next to me. It was a boy around 14 years old with huge, gentle eyes. He told me his name was Jean Pierre.

I WANT MY DADDY.

YOUR FAMILY WILL COME LOOKING FOR YOU. DON'T WORRY.

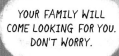

Three days later, Jean Pierre was dead.

Each day was hard and terrible, filled with fear, torture and death. From the moment the sun came up, we were forced to carry heavy packs and weapons, to run, to fight, to kill.

Each group of children had a *commandant* who was in charge. I never knew the name of mine, but I remember his face perfectly. He was very short with a long scar across his cheek. He looked as though he never bathed or shaved.

He gave us bayonets, knives and guns, and showed us how to kill. First, by stabbing banana trees. Then, too often, each other.

Commandant warned us all the time about running away.

IF YOU TRY TO LEAVE, WE WILL KILL YOU.

IF YOU DO RETURN HOME, YOUR FAMILY WILL HATE YOU.

I was scared, but I always knew my parents loved me.

We were hungry and thirsty. We were exhausted, frightened and very sad.

Everything was filthy. We slept on hard straw mats under plastic tarps.

The adults were in larger tents across the way. There was only one woman: the rebel leader's wife. I think her name was Constance.

There were also tents for about a dozen older kids who had been there awhile — they would strut around acting tough.

In the evenings, we were brought trays of cornmeal and beans or cassava leaves. But no one talked to us. No one comforted us.

It went on like that for two weeks: threats, drugs, amputations, killing — and worse. They called it "training."

I was always scared.

I worried my father was angry that I hadn't come home.

I didn't know where I was or who I was with.

K-KRACK!

One day, *Commandant* explained to us that we had a mission: to take over a village.

He told us that the younger kids would go at the very front.

THEY WILL HESITATE TO KILL A CHILD.

THEN YOU CAN SHOOT THEM.

We were forced to take drugs and then piled into a truck that took us to the edge of a small village.

The truck stopped, and everyone jumped off. I was supposed to be at the front but was the last out. Everyone ran toward the village, but I didn't move. I was frightened. I thought about my father; I just wanted to go home.

I looked across a clearing and saw some trees. I didn't think; I just ran toward them as fast as I could, not looking back.

I was so scared. My heart was pounding in my chest, and I couldn't breathe.

I slipped, landing on my knee, and the skin of my shin split open. I remember looking down and seeing the blood and bone, but not feeling anything at all.

I looked back at the truck, but nobody was there. I ran and ran.

I ran for three days.

When I had to rest, I climbed trees and napped in the branches — just a few minutes at a time. When the sun went down, I stayed in the trees, peering through the darkness for lions, for rebels.

I had no water. I ate bananas and plums picked from treetops. I stuffed fruit into the pockets of my grimy pants; the same green shorts I had worn to school the day we were kidnapped. The last day I saw Kevin. His blood was still splattered across my shirt.

All I thought, every moment, was — "Get home."

I could have been running in circles, for all I knew. But I just kept going and going.

On the third day, I heard a loud voice. I dropped down into the long grass, terrified that the rebels had finally caught up to me.

There was the sound of a car slowing to a stop and more voices. But they didn't sound angry. A woman shouted, and then laughed.

I crept closer, crawling on my belly. Through the grass, I could see people coming and going. No one had guns. No one looked scared.

I recognized the building. It was the store in Butembo where we went for ice cream. I ran as fast as I could, screaming for my father. I thought he was inside, waiting for me.

PAPA! PAPA!

I ran to the store owner and fell into his arms, sobbing.

MICHEL!! YOUR FATHER HAS BEEN LOOKING EVERYWHERE FOR YOU!

Then everything went black.

Back home, things went on, but they were never the same.

Nothing like this had ever happened in Beni before. It had been the safest place in the world to be a child, or so people had thought.

Now that I was back, people were nervous and rumors were flying like locusts. Who was responsible? Who could be trusted? Was this a sign of war?

My father told me not to talk about my experience, not even with him or my mother. He wanted to protect me from people who were confused and scared. He also wanted to protect me from myself, from my memories.

THERE ARE MUCH BETTER THINGS IN YOUR LIFE THAN THIS, MICHEL. LOOK TO THE FUTURE.

This was our way. Terrible things sometimes happened; you couldn't dwell on them.

He kept me very close, and I was glad. Like me, he was afraid to be apart, even for a moment.

But nothing could erase what had happened.

I didn't know who I was anymore. I didn't want to play with other children. I didn't want to play at all.

Back at school, everyone knew where I had been. I found a boy taunting my sister one day.

YOUR BROTHER IS A CHILD KILLER!

I was so angry, I jumped on him. I ripped handfuls of grass from the ground, stuffing them into his mouth.

SHUT UP! SHUT UP!

When I got home that day, my father punished me for fighting. Then he held me close.

In the following weeks, he lavished love on me. He bought me toys.

He tried to give me back my childhood.

But he couldn't.

I thought about Kevin every night. I stopped going to school. I was confused and hurting.

My cousins tried to play with me, and I tried to play along. But pretending was impossible.

Eventually, my father took me to stay with his sister in another town for a couple of months.

He wanted me to have a break from the constant worry, the constant memories. He wanted me to be safe.

Those months passed in a blur for me. For my father, however, everything became very clear.

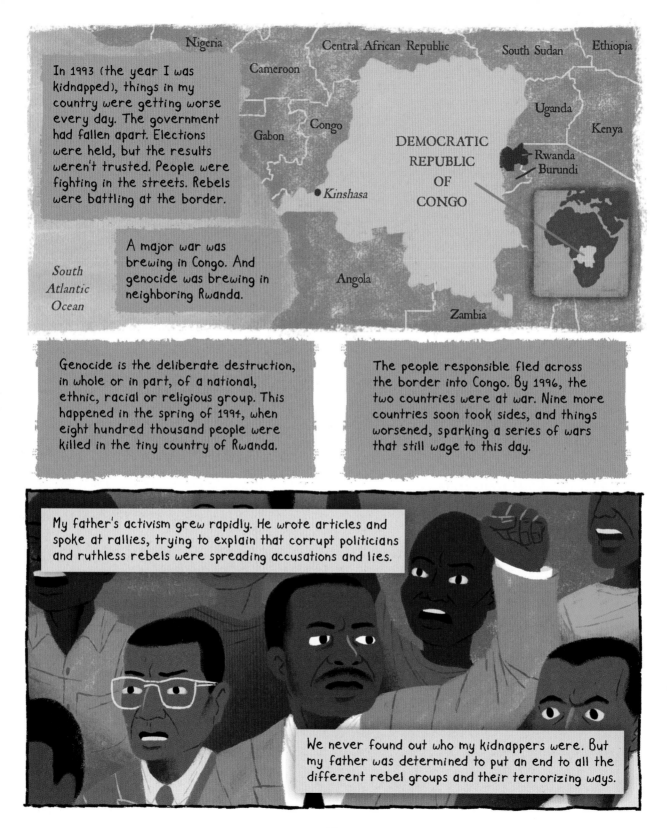

In 1993 (the year I was kidnapped), things in my country were getting worse every day. The government had fallen apart. Elections were held, but the results weren't trusted. People were fighting in the streets. Rebels were battling at the border.

A major war was brewing in Congo. And genocide was brewing in neighboring Rwanda.

Genocide is the deliberate destruction, in whole or in part, of a national, ethnic, racial or religious group. This happened in the spring of 1994, when eight hundred thousand people were killed in the tiny country of Rwanda.

The people responsible fled across the border into Congo. By 1996, the two countries were at war. Nine more countries soon took sides, and things worsened, sparking a series of wars that still wage to this day.

My father's activism grew rapidly. He wrote articles and spoke at rallies, trying to explain that corrupt politicians and ruthless rebels were spreading accusations and lies.

We never found out who my kidnappers were. But my father was determined to put an end to all the different rebel groups and their terrorizing ways.

HOW CAN A GROUP THAT CALLS ITSELF "THE MOVEMENT FOR THE LIBERATION OF CONGO" BURN DOWN OUR SCHOOLS, STEAL OUR MEDICINE AND ATTACK OUR PEOPLE?

I was eight years old now, but it was all still so confusing.

Like before, my father tried to explain things to me. What he told me was no longer just about faraway times and places; now it was about us.

He explained that the rebels were angry with him, and he may be sent to jail.

IF THIS HAPPENS, MICHEL, I WILL NEED YOU. YOU MUST COME TO THE PRISON, AND I'LL SNEAK YOU RECORDINGS TO DELIVER. PEOPLE MUST CONTINUE TO HEAR THE TRUTH!

THE REBELS MAY TRY TO KILL YOU! AREN'T YOU AFRAID?

MICHEL, NEVER FEAR DEATH. DEATH COMES TO EVERYONE. WHAT MATTERS IS WHAT YOU DO WITH THE TIME YOU HAVE.

THIS IS WHAT DEFINES YOU: THE LEGACY THAT YOU LEAVE, NOT JUST FOR YOUR FAMILY BUT FOR THE WHOLE WORLD.

At the time, I didn't fully understand. I just rolled my eyes at him because he sounded so corny. Yet, these lessons have stayed in my head.

33

When I turned 10, my father was kidnapped. For months he was tortured, until a priest helped him escape to Uganda.

The rebel soldiers came to our house, looking for him.

ARF! ARF!

TA-TA-TAK!!

I remember that day very well. I was doing math homework in my room when I heard gunshots.

I dove under my bed, feeling sick and shaking, seeing Kevin's face in front of me. I heard my mother and sisters downstairs, screaming.

Suddenly, I remembered my father's words.

IF I AM EVER FORCED TO LEAVE, MICHEL, YOU MUST PROTECT THE FAMILY.

Taking a deep breath, I crawled from under the bed and crept to the door. I froze there, terrified, thinking, "I'm only a kid! What am I supposed to do?"

CLICK!

A rebel held his gun to my head. Others were holding my mother and sisters down on the living room floor.

IF YOU CLOSE YOUR EYES, I WILL SHOOT YOU.

I thought to myself, "If they are going to kill me, then they should do it now!"

I jumped on one of them and punched him again and again. He pulled me off and shoved me against the wall.

I could hear my mother and sisters crying, and the other soldiers laughing. He lifted his machete to cut my throat, but then he stopped. He slowly sliced it across my cheek.

The rebels knew that making us suffer would hurt my father even more than if we were dead.

My father had been collecting proof of the terrible things the rebels were doing and then writing articles and giving speeches about them.

HE IS SCARING AWAY THOSE WHO SUPPORT US, AND WE ARE LOSING MONEY. HE MUST STOP, UNDERSTAND?

They burned my father's notes, tore up his books and smashed the recordings he had made.

Our family fled in fear. Vicky and Viviane ran away before we could stop them. In despair, my mother took Marizia and me to Northern Uganda in the back of a truck, to try to join my father at a makeshift refugee camp.

It was a three-day trip on bumpy roads, squashed in with many other frightened refugees. We had nothing but one bottle of cola to drink and a loaf of bread to eat.

But the joy on my father's face when we found each other made me forget our problems. Love made everything okay again. For that moment, anyway.

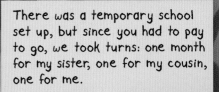

There was a temporary school set up, but since you had to pay to go, we took turns: one month for my sister, one for my cousin, one for me.

In the refugee camp, we had nothing. We had left everything behind. We slept all together in a plastic tent; we had no bed, no blankets or pillows. We were given a bag of rice and beans, and that was the only food we ate.

There was nothing to do. I thought a lot about revenge, that maybe I should start a rebel group. And even though I knew that would make me just as bad as them, the anger I felt was eating me up.

But soon that started to change.

Each night, everyone in the camp would sit together and talk. A man told us how rebel soldiers had cut off his arms. That was the first time I had ever seen a grown man cry. A woman told us that she had walked for six weeks to get here, eating nothing but mangoes and bananas.

Listening to stories like these night after night, I began to realize that everyone there had gone through horrible things, just like me. I thought, "This must be normal, so I shouldn't feel sorry for myself."

Some stories I heard around the fire never made sense: the ones people told about North America. We hoped to immigrate there one day and escape the violence of home.

People said that huge trucks like the ones that brought food to our camp were driven just for fun. That a man named Michael Jordan was paid $30 million dollars to throw a ball into a basket. And, weirdest of all, that people paid hundreds of dollars to go to a park to see a giant mouse with big ears.

YEAH, RIGHT! WHO WOULD PAY TO SEE A BIG MOUSE?

Six years later, Mom, Marizia and I were finally allowed to move to Canada.

My older sisters stayed behind. The refugee laws at that time only allowed children under eighteen to go with their parents. Vicky made her own refugee claim and joined us a couple of years later. But Viviane never made it out. Neither did my father.

We have never found out what happened to my sister, but we know my father was poisoned by his enemies before we left Uganda.

I'll always remember his dying words.

REMEMBER, MICHEL, A GREAT PERSON IS NOT DESCRIBED BY THEIR MONEY OR SUCCESS ...

... BUT RATHER BY THEIR HEART AND WHAT THEY DO FOR OTHERS.

I have lived in North America for ten years now.

When I first arrived, I thought people here didn't care about the troubles in other countries.

... HATE MY NEW PHONE ...

... SUCH A STUPID CLASS ...

... PIZZA WAS ICE-COLD BY THE TIME ...

... MAKING ME TAKE PIANO ...

... TOLD MY MOM TO JUST LEAVE ME ALONE ...

... HATE SCHOOL ...

But now I know that young people here just don't understand what is happening right now, to kids just like them.

So I share my story, as painful as it is for me to tell and as sad as it is for you to hear. In doing so, I have discovered that people do care! I am part of a movement of young people who want to help, who are passionate and who will take action so that what happened to me will not happen to the children of the future.

Working together, we will make positive changes in the world. As my father used to tell me, "If you ever think you are too small to make a difference, try sleeping in a room with a mosquito."

MORE ABOUT MICHEL

When Michel arrived in Canada at 16 years old, he had a lot to deal with: a new school, a new language, a new country. Plus, he had made a promise to his dad to keep his family together.

So, after school each day, Michel worked three jobs: as a cleaner first in an office building, then in a hospital, and then in a furniture store. Finally, at midnight, he would go home to get some sleep before school started again the next day. He was trying to earn enough money to bring his older sisters to Canada.

But before he could save enough, his sister Viviane disappeared, never to be heard from again. Michel was heartbroken. Although he eventually helped his other sister, Vicky, make it to Canada, he still felt that he had broken his promise to his father.

Michel was having a hard time coping. A kind teacher asked him if it would help to talk about his grief and his challenges as a refugee. She suggested he join a group of young international public speakers.

Michel didn't like to talk about himself much, but he found discussing the issues that mattered to him really did help. He began to open up, little by little, and made good friends as a result.

Michel has worked long and hard to heal from his experience as a child soldier. It is a label that was forced on him, but it is only a very small part of who he is. Michel is a student, an activist and an athlete. Today, along with researching root causes of poverty and conflict, Michel continues to share his powerful and inspiring message of hope with people all over the world.

What Is a Child Soldier?

The official definition of a child soldier is **anyone under 18 years old who is used by an armed group in any way, including boys and girls used as fighters, cooks, porters, messengers, spies or for sexual purposes.**

While over 100 countries have formally agreed on this definition, many have not. But getting everyone in the world to agree takes time, even when it's about something so wrong.

Omar Khadr is a Canadian who was living in Afghanistan with his father (a member of the al-Qaeda terrorist group) when he was shot and captured by American Forces after a battle in 2002. Though he was only 15 years old, Omar Khadr was sent to the American military prison camp in Guantánamo Bay, Cuba. He was held there for eight years without a trial, accused of killing an American soldier by throwing a hand grenade. Eventually he pleaded guilty and is now in jail in Canada. Still today, people do not agree if he should have been imprisoned because he was a child at the time of the battle. This case has divided people and governments all around the world.

How Many Child Soldiers Are There?

It is hard to know the exact number of child soldiers, but an estimated 250 000 children under the age of 18 are currently serving in government armed forces or armed rebel groups. Of that number, it is estimated that over 40 percent are girls.

Joseph Kony is the leader of a very violent rebel group that has terrorized Uganda and surrounding countries for decades. Over the years, as many as 500 to 1000 children have been abducted (taken by force) annually into Kony's Lord's Resistance Army, which was thought to be made up of 90 percent child soldiers at times.

Where Are Child Soldiers Used?

We know from Michel's story that children are used as soldiers in the Democratic Republic of Congo. Overall, Africa is home to half of the world's child soldiers. The other estimated 125 000 children are used by militaries and armed groups around the world — in Asia, Latin America, Europe and the Middle East.

With their parents' permission, children as young as 16 or 17 years old are allowed to join the armed forces in many countries, including Canada, the United States, Japan and Britain. As well, children in these countries are sometimes recruited into armed gangs and other violent criminal groups. So you see, the problem is not limited to one part of the world.

How Are Child Soldiers Used?

Child soldiers have four main roles.

Fighters — Because so many weapons today are light and easy to use, children can participate in armed battle. But children may also be used as fighters without weapons. For example, child soldiers are often sent out in front of adult troops, so they are the ones who get shot first, or step on and explode hidden bombs. They are also used as decoys (to trick enemy soldiers out of hiding) or as human shields (because a combatant might not shoot at someone holding a child).

Cooks and Porters — Child soldiers often do the hard and boring work no one else wants to do. For example, they might cook meals for the camp; do the cleaning up; lug water; and carry packs, bedding, food, tents, firewood or other supplies.

Messengers and Spies — Because most people are not suspicious of children, child soldiers are often used to deliver secret messages or to spy on enemies.

Sexual Purposes — Child soldiers, especially girls, are often sexually abused. The effects of this abuse last long after the war is over. Many cultures blame the victims of sexual violence and will not allow them (or their babies) back into their communities.

Why Are Children Used as Soldiers?

According to the United Nations Convention on the Rights of the Child, a child is any person under the age of 18, and all children have the right to protection, to attend school, to live with their families, and all children have the right to play. Using children as soldiers violates every one of these rights. So why does it happen?

There are three main factors that have contributed to the alarming rise in the use of child soldiers over the past few decades.

First, with the invention of small arms it became physically possible for children to use dangerous weapons. Modern guns like the AK-47 are light and simple enough for a child to carry and use.

Second, there has been a huge rise in the number of orphans. Many children have lost their parents to war or disease. (For example, in Africa, AIDS has left tens of millions orphaned over the last two generations.) Orphans are far easier to abduct.

Third, in recent years many countries have suffered from major instability. As you read in Michel's story, conflicts can cause governments to fall apart, schools to close, people to flee and communities to break up. Other things can make a country unstable, too, such as widespread disease, drought and poverty. When a country isn't running properly, surviving each day is difficult and people get desperate. Desperation can make people do things they wouldn't normally, such as using children in battle.

There are lots of reasons why ruthless adults, like those who abducted Michel, would want to use children as soldiers:

- Children are smaller and less experienced than adults, so they are easier to overpower and might be too young to resist.
- Children are more likely to be obedient. At home, at school and pretty much everywhere, children must do as they are told, even when they disagree or don't understand.
- Children are often more easily brainwashed and manipulated than adults.
- An adult soldier might not want to fight

a child. In fact, a conflict involving child soldiers can sometimes prevent other countries from getting involved.

What Is Being Done to Help?

Frustratingly, there is no simple solution for stopping the use of child soldiers. However, people are trying to make a positive difference in a number of ways.

Global Level

The United Nations (UN) is strongly pushing governments to make their armed forces child-free. The UN's Children, Not Soldiers campaign is working to end the use of children by the national armies of seven countries. But this still leaves about 50 non-government armed groups using children as soldiers. The UN has added these groups to a List of Shame, hoping that other UN member countries will pressure them to stop.

The International Criminal Court (ICC) has called for the arrest of several commanders known to recruit child soldiers. The challenge is that the ICC does not have its own police force to capture them.

The United Nations was formed at the end of the Second World War to promote and protect world peace. Almost all the countries in the world are part of the UN, and together they agree to rules that everyone is supposed to follow.

The International Criminal Court was formed in 2002 to bring to justice anyone accused of the most serious crimes of international concern (such as genocide and crimes against humanity).

Country Level

Some countries know child soldiers are being used within their borders and are committed to stopping it. For example, Sierra Leone is training its national military and police in ways to keep children from being recruited as soldiers, as well as how to protect child soldiers they may encounter. The government of Colombia is helping former child soldiers return home at the end of a conflict. They send a trained adult to help each child fit back into his or her community. They also protect the children from returning to military activity.

The main thing a country can do to prevent the use of child soldiers is make sure that its own armed forces do not use children. Three-quarters of the world's countries (about 175) have laws that state no one under the age of 18 can be forced to join their armed forces. And half of all countries (about 100) have laws stating that no one under the age of 18 can volunteer. Also, many countries have laws prohibiting anyone in their country from using children in war, even outside of their national armies (for instance, rebel groups).

Another thing a country can do is put pressure on the countries using child soldiers. They do this through diplomacy (talking to them), trade embargoes (refusing to buy and sell with them) or war.

Ground Level

Many charities called non-governmental organizations (NGOs) work to prevent (stop), disarm (take guns away from), demobilize (rescue), rehabilitate (heal) and reintegrate (bring home) child soldiers.

There are hundreds of these NGOs working in their local communities all around the world.

Here are a few of them:

- The **ASO (Association de Soutien de l'Opprime)** in the Democratic Republic of Congo works with local artists in Goma and Bukavu to help ex–child soldiers use dance, drama, music, arts and crafts to heal their trauma while learning new skills.

- **SIEMBRA** in Colombia works with children to prevent gang recruitment. One of its projects helps kids in different areas share their personal stories in a traveling newspaper. By learning about each other, they are less likely to fight against one another in gangs.

- **Local Demobilization and Reintegration Committees**, made up of community leaders and locally based NGOs in Afghanistan, help release children from armed forces and then provide them with education or job training.

There are also NGOs that work internationally:

- **Child Soldiers International** monitors (watches closely) the use of child soldiers in Chad, the Democratic Republic of Congo, Myanmar, Thailand and the United Kingdom. It also works to end the recruitment of children and pressures governments to release active child soldiers.

- Since only governments can sign UN agreements, an organization called **Geneva Call** works closely with rebels and other non-state armed groups to inform them about international laws, rights and rules (such as not using children as soldiers). Then, these groups sign agreements promising to follow these rules.

- The **Roméo Dallaire Child Soldiers Initiative** works to prevent the use of child soldiers before it starts by training militaries and police around the world in ways to stop armed groups from recruiting children. It also creates educational comics and radio programs to share ideas with communities for protecting themselves and their children. And it does groundbreaking research: it recently uncovered the use of children as pirates in Somalia.

- **War Child** works to protect children who live in war zones and conflict-affected places. It builds schools and helps former child soldiers, especially girls, rejoin their communities in the Democratic Republic of Congo and Uganda.

What Can YOU Do?

Remember what Michel's father used to tell him? "If you ever think you are too small to make a difference, try sleeping in a room with a mosquito." Here are three kinds of actions you can take to help make a difference:

Education —— Learn and Share!

Read as much as you can about the issue. Find out what your country's government is doing about child soldiers. Learn about products such as coltan, diamonds, chocolate and oil, and how our desire to live a comfortable life affects other places in the world.

Pass this book on to a friend or share what you've learned with your class. Discuss the issue with your teachers, classmates, family and friends, and brainstorm possible solutions.

Activism and Advocacy —— Get Involved!

Use your voice — write to or email your local politicians or your country's leaders. Let them know what your concerns are.

Help out a local NGO. There might be things you can do at home with your family or at school with your class that will help their work.

Raising awareness is another great way to get involved. Consider joining the international Red Hand Day protest. Every February 12, children all around the world paint their hands red to show support for ending the use of child soldiers. (February 12 is the day the UN Optional Protocol on the Involvement of Children in Armed Conflict made it illegal for anyone under the age of 18 to be used in armed conflict.)

Or you might participate in We Are Silent, a Free the Children campaign that takes place every April. It encourages you to stay quiet for 24 hours (that means no talking or texting!) while wearing a T-shirt that explains the issue you are passionate about. For example, your shirt might say, "I am silent to recognize the 250 000 children who are being used as child soldiers."

Philanthropy — Raise Money!

You've learned about the issue. You've spread the word. Now, you can do something to make a concrete change — hold a fundraiser for the charity of your choice. All charities need money to do their important work, and most have websites with helpful suggestions and resources for planning your event.

There are lots of fun ways to raise funds! Take pledges for each red hand your school collects or for each hour of your vow of silence. Hold a dance where kids donate a dollar to request a song. Get your whole school involved in a silly competition — maybe the teacher of the class that raises the most donations has to wear a funny costume for a day. Or maybe everyone donates a dollar to come to school in their pajamas.

These events can take some planning and hard work, but it will be worth it as you raise funds and awareness. The more people who know about Michel's story, and the hundreds of thousands like it, the more people will care. And the more people who care, the more change will be possible.

Be the change you want to see in the world!

PRIMARY SOURCES FOR FURTHER RESEARCH

If you want to learn more about child soldiers and other topics raised in this book, these are some valuable sources:

The United Nations Convention on the Rights of the Child (child-friendly version), **www.unicef.ca/sites/ default/files/imce_uploads/child_ friendly_crc_ncd_en.pdf**

Impact of Armed Conflict on Children (UN report by Graça Machel), **www.unicef.org/graca/**

The Paris Principles: Principles and Guidelines on Children Associated with Armed Forces or Armed Groups (includes the definition of "child soldier"), **www.unicef.org/emerg/files/ ParisPrinciples310107English.pdf**

Acknowledgments:

Loving thanks to our families, as well as Jamie Altena, Anthoula Bourolias, Craig and Mandy Buckles, Roméo Dallaire, Alana Kapell, Nicole Levesque and St. Patrick's Catholic High School in Ottawa, Abigail Pugh, Stacey Roderick, Eduardo Garcia Rolland, Joanne Schwartz, Bronwyn Singleton, Tanya Zayed and above all to the memory of Ramazani Chikwanine, whose passion and commitment to human rights was passed on to his children who continue his legacy. — JDH & MC

CitizenKid™ is a trademark of Kids Can Press Ltd.

Text © 2015 Jessica Dee Humphreys and Michel Chikwanine
Illustrations © 2015 Claudia Dávila

Kids Can Press acknowledges the financial support of the Government of Ontario, through the Ontario Media Development Corporation's Ontario Book Initiative; the Ontario Arts Council; the Canada Council for the Arts; and the Government of Canada, through the CBF, for our publishing activity.

Published in Canada by
Kids Can Press Ltd.
25 Dockside Drive
Toronto, ON M5A 0B5

Published in the U.S. by
Kids Can Press Ltd.
2250 Military Road
Tonawanda, NY 14150

Photo on page 42 by Twice Research Institute co, Ltd.

www.kidscanpress.com

Edited by Stacey Roderick
Designed by Marie Bartholomew

This book is smyth sewn casebound. Manufactured in Malaysia in 3/2015 by Tien Wah Press (Pte.) Ltd.

CM 15 0 9 8 7 6 5 4 3 2 1

FSC
www.fsc.org
MIX
Paper from responsible sources
FSC® C012700

Library and Archives Canada Cataloguing in Publication

Humphreys, Jessica Dee, author
    Child soldier : when boys and girls are used in war / written by Jessica Dee Humphreys & Michel Chikwanine ; illustrated by Claudia Dávila.

(CitizenKid)
For ages 10–14.

ISBN 978-1-77138-126-0 (bound)

1. Chikwanine, Michel — Childhood and youth — Comic books, strips, etc. 2. Chikwanine, Michel — Childhood and youth — Juvenile literature. 3. Child soldiers — Congo (Democratic Republic) — Comic books, strips, etc. 4. Child soldiers — Congo (Democratic Republic) — Juvenile literature. 5. Congo (Democratic Republic) — History — 1997– — Comic books, strips, etc. 6. Congo (Democratic Republic) — History — 1997– — Juvenile literature. 7. Children and war — Comic books, strips, etc. 8. Children and war — Juvenile literature. 9. Graphic novels. I. Chikwanine, Michel, author II. Dávila, Claudia, illustrator III. Title. IV. Series: CitizenKid

UB419.C75H86 2015   j355.0083'096751   C2014-907064-0

Kids Can Press is a **l̃O̧ŗÚŞ**™ Entertainment company